# Night and Day

by Gordon Gedling

# Night

Dusk is the start of the night.

# Day

Dawn is the start of the day.

# Night

The night is dark.

# Day

The day is light.

# Night

The sun does not shine at night.

# Day

The sun shines in the day.

# Day

Cold lemonade

The day is warm.

Some animals sleep at night.

# Day

We are awake in the day.

# Night

We dream at night.

# Day

We daydream in the day.

# INDEX

**The numbers tell you on which pages you'll find the words.**

Animals 10, 11
Awake 13
Cool 8
Dark 4
Dawn 2
Daydream 15
Dream 14
Dusk 3
Light 5
Sleep 10, 11, 12
Sun 6, 7
ZZZZ! 10, 11, 12